A collection of Data Science Interview Questions Solved in Python and Spark

Hands-on Big Data and Machine Learning (volume I)

Antonio Gulli

"Data Science" is the sixth of a series of 25 Chapters devoted to algorithms, problem solving, machine learning, big data and C++/Python programming.

DEDICATION

To Lorenzo, Leonardo, Aurora and Francesca

"I heard there was a secret chord
That David played and it pleased the Lord
But you don't really care for music, do ya?"

[Leonard Cohen, 1984]

"La tua bocca si apre al sorriso e la tua mano ad aiutare gli altri"

ACKNOWLEDGMENTS

Thanks to Eric, Francesco, Michele, Dario, Domenico, Carla, Antonio, Ettore, Federica, Laura, Antonella, Susana, and Antonello for their friendship.

Table of Contents

1. What are the most important machine learning techniques?

Solution

In his famous essay *"Computing Machinery and Intelligence"* Alan Turing asked a fundamental question *"Can machines do what we (as thinking entities) can do?"* Machine learning is not about thinking but more about a related activity: **Learning** or better, according to Arthur Samuel, the *"Field of study that gives computers the ability to learn without being explicitly programmed"*.

Machine learning techniques are typically classified into two categories:

In **supervised learning** pairs of examples made up by *(inputs, desired output)* are available and the computer learns a model according to which given an input, a desired output with a minimal error is predicted. Classification, Neural Networks and Regression are all examples of supervised learning. For all techniques we assume that there is an oracle or a teacher that can teach to computers what to do in order for them to apply the learned lessons on new unseen data.

In **unsupervised learning** computers have no teachers and they are left alone in searching for structures, patterns and anomalies in data. Clustering and Density Estimations are typical examples of unsupervised machine learning.

Let us now review the main machine learning techniques:

In **classification** the teacher presents pairs of *(inputs, target classes)* and the computer learns to attribute classes to new unseen data. Naïve Bayesian, SVM, Decision Trees and Neural Networks are all classification methodologies. The first two are discussed in this volume, while the remaining ones will be part of the next volume.

In **Regression** the teacher presents pairs of *(inputs, continuous targets)* and computers learn how to predict continuous values on new and unseen data. Linear and Logistic regression are examples which will be discussed in the present volume. Decision Trees, SVM and Neural Networks can also be used for Regression.

In **Associative rule learning** computers are presented with a large set of observations, all being made up of multiple variables. The task is then to learn relations between variables such us A & B →C (if A and B happen, then C will also happen).

In **Clustering** computers learn how to partition observations in various subsets, so that each partition will be made up of similar observations according to some well-defined metric. Algorithms like K-Means and DBSCAN belong also to this class.

In **Density estimation** computers learn how to find statistical values that describe data. Algorithms like Expectation Maximization belong also to this class.

2. Why is it important to have a robust set of metrics for machine learning?

Solution

Any machine learning technique should be evaluated by using metrics for analytically assessing the quality of results. For instance: if we need to categorize objects such as people, movies or songs into different classes, *precision* and *recall* might be suitable metrics.

Precision is the ratio $\dfrac{tp}{tp + fp}$ where tp is the number of true positives and fp is the number of false positives. **Recall** is the ratio $\dfrac{tp}{tp + fn}$ where tp is the number of true positives and fn is the number of false negatives. True and false are attributes derived by using manually created data. Precision and Recall are typically reported in a 2-d graph known as P/R Curves, where different algorithmic graphs can be compared by reporting the achieved Precision for fixed values of Recall.

In addition, F1 is another frequently used metric, which combines Precision and Recall into a single value:

$$F1 = \frac{2 * precision * recall}{precision + recall}$$

Scikit-learn provides a comprehensive set of metrics for classification, clustering, regression, ranking and pairwise judgment[1]. As an example the code below computes Precision and Recall.

Code

```
import numpy as np
from sklearn.metrics import precision_recall_curve
y_true = np.array([0,1,1,0, 1])
y_scores = np.array([0.5, 0.6, 0.38, 0.9, 1])
precision, recall, thresholds = precision_recall_curve(y_true, y_scores)
print precision
print recall
```

3. Why are Features extraction and engineering so important in machine learning?

Solution

The Features are the selected variables for making predictions. For instance, suppose you'd like to forecast whether tomorrow there will be a sunny day then you will probably pick features like humidity (a numerical value), speed of wind (another numeric value), some historical information (what happened during the last few years), whether or not it is sunny today (a categorical value yes/no) and a few other features. Your choice can dramatically impact on your model for the same algorithm and you need to run multiple experiments in order to find what the right amount of data and what the right features are in order to forecast with minimal error. It is not unusual to have problems represented by thousands of features and combinations of them and a good feature engineer will use tools for stack ranking features according to their contribution in reducing the error for prediction.

Different authors use different names for different features including attributes, variables and predictors. In this book we consistently use features.

---

[1] http://scikit-learn.org/stable/modules/classes.html#module-sklearn.metrics

Features can be *categorical* such as marital status, gender, state of residence, place of birth, or *numerical* such as age, income, height and weight. This distinction is important because certain algorithms such as *linear regression* work only with numerical attributes and if categorical features are present, they need to be somehow encoded into numerical values.

In other words, feature engineering is the art of extracting, selecting and transforming essential characteristics representing data. It is sometimes considered less glamourous than machine learning algorithms but in reality any experienced Data Scientist knows that a simple algorithm on a well-chosen set of features performs better than a sophisticated algorithm on a not so good set of features.

Also simple algorithms are frequently easier to implement in a distributed way and therefore they scale well with large datasets. So the rule of thumb is in what Galileo already said many centuries ago: *"Simplicity is the ultimate sophistication"*. Pick your algorithm carefully and spend a lot of time in investigating your data and in creating meaningful summaries with appropriate feature engineering.

Real world objects are complex and features are used to analytically represent those objects. From one hand this representation has an inherent error which can be reduced by carefully selecting a right set of representatives. From the other hand we might not want to create a too complex representation because it might be computationally expensive for the machine to learn a sophisticate model, indeed such model could possibly not generalize well to the unseen data.

Real world data is noisy. We might have very few instances (outliers) which show a sensible difference from the majority of the remaining data, while the selected algorithm should be resilient enough to outliers.

Real world data might have redundant information. When we extract features, we might be interested in optimizing simplicity of learned models and discard new features which show a high correlation with the already observed ones.

ETL is the process of Extraction, Transformation and Loading of features from real data for creating various learning sets. Transformation in particular refers to operations such as features weighting, high correlated features discarding, the creation of synthetic features derivative of the one observed in the data and the reduction of high dimension features space into a lower one by using either hashing or rather sophisticate space projection techniques. For example in this book we discuss:

- TFxIDF, an example of features weighting used in text classification
- ChiSquare, an example of filtering of highly correlated features
- Kernel Trick, an example of creation of derivative features
- Hashing, a simple technique to reduce feature space dimensions
- Binning, an example of transformation of continuous features into a discrete one. New synthetic features might be created in order to represent the bins.

4. Can you provide an example of features extraction?

Solution

Let's suppose that we want to perform machine learning on textual files. The first step is to extract meaningful feature vectors from a text. A typical representation is the so called *bag of words* where:

a) Each word w in the text collection is associated with a unique integer $j = wordId(w)$ assigned to it.

b) For each document i, the number of occurrences of each word w is computed and this value is stored in a matrix $M(i, j)$. Please, note that M is typically a sparse matrix because when a word is not present in a document, its count will be zero.

Numpy, Scikit-learn and Spark all support sparse vectors[2]. Let's see an example where we start to load a dataset made up of Usenet articles[3] where the *alt.atheism* category is considered and the collection of text documents is converted into a matrix of token counts. We then print the $wordId('man')$.

Code

```
from sklearn.datasets import fetch_20newsgroups
```

---

[2] http://docs.scipy.org/doc/scipy/reference/sparse.html

[3] http://scikit-learn.org/stable/datasets/

```
from sklearn.feature_extraction.text import CountVectorizer
categories = ['alt.atheism']
newsgroups_train = fetch_20newsgroups(subset='train',
categories=categories)
count_vect = CountVectorizer()
Train_counts = count_vect.fit_transform(newsgroups_train.data)
print count_vect.vocabulary_.get(u'man')
```

5. What is a training set, a validation set, a test set and a gold set in supervised and unsupervised learning?

Solution

In machine learning a set of true labels is called the *gold set*. This set of examples is typically built manually either by human experts or via crowdsourcing with tools like the Amazon Mechanical Turk[4] or via explicit/implicit feedback collected by users online. For instance: a gold set can contain news articles that are manually assigned to different categories by experts of the various subjects, or it might contain movies with associated rating provided by Netflix users, or ratings of images collected via crowdsourcing.

Supervised machine learning consists of four phases:

   a. *Training phase*: A sample extracted by the gold set is used to learn a family of data models. Each model can be generated from this family by choosing an appropriate set of hyper-parameters, i.e. factors which can be used for algorithms fine-tuning s;
   b. *Validation phase*: The best learned model is selected from the family by picking hyper-parameters which minimize a computed error function on a gold set sample called "validation set"; This phase is used for identifying the best configuration for a given algorithm;
   c. *Test phase:* The error for the best learned model is evaluated on a gold set sample called "test set". This phase is useful for comparing models built by adopting different algorithms;
   d. *Application phase:* The learned model is applied to the real-world data.

---

[4] https://www.mturk.com/mturk/welcome

Two additional observations can be here highlighted: first, the training set, the validation set and the test set are all sampled from the same gold set but those samples are independent. Second, it has been assumed that the learned model can be described by means of two different functions f and h combined by using a set of hyper-parameters λ.

Unsupervised machine learning consists in tests and application phases only because there is no model to be learned a-priori. In fact unsupervised algorithms adapt dynamically to the observed data.

6. What is a Bias - Variance tradeoff?

Solution

Bias and Variance are two independent sources of errors for machine learning which prevent algorithms to generalize the models learned beyond the training set.

- *Bias* is the error representing missing relations between features and outputs. In machine learning this phenomenon is called *underfitting.*
- *Variance* is the error representing sensitiveness to small training data fluctuations. In machine learning this phenomenon is called *overfitting.*

A good learning algorithm should capture patterns in the training data (low bias), but it should also generalize well with unseen application data (low variance). In general, a complex model can show low bias because it captures many relations in the training data and, at the same time, it can show high variance because it will not necessarily generalize well. The opposite happens with models with high bias and low variance. In many algorithms an error can be analytically decomposed in three components: bias, variance and the irreducible error representing a lower bound on the expected error for unseen sample data.

One way to reduce the variance is to try to get more data or to decrease the complexity of a model. One way to reduce the bias is to add more features or to make the model more complex, as adding more data will not help in this case. Finding the right balance between Bias and Variance is an art that every Data scientist must be able to manage.

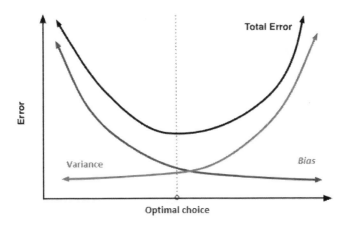

7. What is a cross-validation and what is an overfitting?

Solution

Learning a model on a set of examples and testing it on the same set is a logical mistake because the model would have no errors on the test set but it will almost certainly have a poor performance on the real application data. This problem is called **overfitting** and it is the reason why the gold set is typically split into independent sets for training, validation and test. An example of random split is reported in the code section, where a toy dataset with diabetics' data has been randomly split into two parts: the training set and the test set.

Given a family of learned models, the validation set is used for estimating the best hyper-parameters. However, by adopting this strategy there is still the risk that the hyper-parameters overfit a particular validation set.

The solution to this problem is called **cross-validation**. The idea is simple: the test set is split in k smaller sets called folds and the model is then learned on $k-1$ folds, while the remaining data is used for validation. This process is repeated in a loop and the metrics achieved for each iteration are averaged. An example of cross validation is reported in the section below where our toy dataset is classified via SVM and accuracy is computed via cross-validation. SVM is a classification technique and "accuracy" is a quality measurement (the number of correct predictions made, divided by the total number of predictions made and multiplied by 100 to turn it into a percentage).

Stratified KFold is a variation of *k-fold* where each set contains approximately the same balanced percentage of samples for each target class as the complete set.

Code

```
import numpy as np
from sklearn import cross_validation
from sklearn import datasets
from sklearn import svm
diabets = datasets.load_diabetes()
X_train, X_test, y_train, y_test = \
cross_validation.train_test_split(
    diabets.data, diabets.target, test_size=0.2, random_state=0)
print X_train.shape, y_train.shape  # test size 20%
print X_test.shape, y_test.shape
clf = svm.SVC(kernel='linear', C=1)
scores = cross_validation.cross_val_score(
    clf, diabets.data, diabets.target, cv=4) # 4-folds
print scores
print("Accuracy: %0.2f (+/- %0.2f)" % (scores.mean(), scores.std()))
```

8. Why are vectors and norms used in machine learning?

Solution

Objects such as movies, songs and documents are typically represented by means of vectors of features. Those features are a synthetic summary of the most salient and discriminative objects characteristics.

Given a collection of vectors (the so-called vector space) V, a norm on V is a function $p: V \rightarrow R$ satisfying the following properties: For all complex numbers a and all $u, v \in V$,

1. $p(av) = |a| \, p(v)$
2. $p(u + v) \leq p(u) + p(v)$
3. $If \, p(v) = 0$ then **v** is the zero vector

The intuitive notion of length for a vector is captured by the norm 2

$$||x||_2 = \sqrt{x_1^2 + \dots + x_n^2}$$

More generally we have the norm p

$$||x||_p = (\sum_{i=1}^{n} |x_i|^p)^{\frac{1}{p}}$$

The special case of infinity norm is $||x||_\infty$ is defined as

$$||x||_\infty = \max_i |x_i|$$

Code

```
from numpy import linalg as LA
import numpy as np
a = np.arange(22)
print LA.norm(a)
print LA.norm(a, 1)
```

9. What are Numpy, Scipy and Spark essential datatypes?

Solution

Numpy provides efficient support for memorizing vectors and matrices and for linear algebra operations[5]. For instance: $dot(a, b[, out])$ is the dot product of two vectors, while $inner(a, b)$ and $outer(a, b[, out])$ are respectively the inner and outer products.

Scipy provides support for sparse matrices and vectors with multiple memorization strategies in order to save space when dealing with zero entries.[6] In particular the COOrdinate format specifies the non-zero v value for the coordinates(i, j), while the Compressed Sparse Colum matrix (CSC) satisfies the relationship $M[row\_ind[k], col\_ind[k]] = data[k]$

Spark has many native datatypes for local and distributed computations. The primary data abstraction is a distributed collection of items called "Resilient Distributed Dataset (**RDD**)". RDDs can be created from Hadoop InputFormats[7]

[5] http://docs.scipy.org/doc/numpy/reference/routines.linalg.html

[6] http://docs.scipy.org/doc/scipy/reference/sparse.html

[7]http://hadoop.apache.org/docs/r2.6.0/api/org/apache/hadoop/mapred/InputFormat.html

or by transforming other RDDs. Numpy arrays, Python list and Scipy CSC sparse matrices are all supported. In addition: MLIB, the Spark library for machine learning, supports *SparseVectors* and *LabeledPoint*, i.e. local vectors, either dense or sparse, associated with a label/response

Code

```
import numpy as np
from scipy.sparse import csr_matrix
M = csr_matrix([[4, 1, 0], [4, 0, 3], [0, 0, 1]])

from pyspark.mllib.linalg import SparseVector
from pyspark.mllib.regression import LabeledPoint
label = 0.0
point = LabeledPoint(label, SparseVector(3, [0, 2], [1.0, 3.0]))

textRDD = sc.textFile("README.md")
print textRDD.count() # count items in RDD
```

10.Can you provide an example for Map and Reduce in Spark? (Let's compute the Mean Square Error)

Solution

Spark is a powerful paradigm for parallel computations which are mapped into multiple servers with no need of dealing with low level operations such as scheduling, data partitioning, communication and recovery. Those low level operations were typically exposed to the programmers by previous paradigms. Now Spark solves these problems on our behalf.

A simple form of parallel computation supported by Spark is the "Map and Reduce" which has been made popular by Google[8].

---

[8] http://research.google.com/archive/mapreduce.html

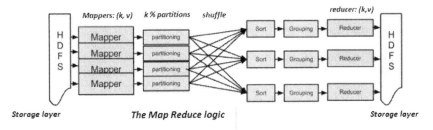

Mappers receive (key, value) pairs and output (key, value)
Partitioners split the keys into partitions and then shuffle the data
Sorters perform the grouping
Reducers receive (key, iterable[value]) and output (key, value)

In this framework a set of keywords is mapped into a number of workers (e.g. parallel servers available for computation) and the results are then reduced (e.g. collected) by applying a "reduce" operator. The reduce operator could be very simple (for instance a sum) or sophisticated (e.g. a user defined function).

As an example of distributed computation let's compute the Mean Square Error (MSE), the average of the squares of the difference between the estimator and what is estimated. In the following example we suppose that valuesAndPreds is an RDD of many $(v_i = true\ labels, p_i = predictions)$ tuples. Those are mapped into values $(v_i - p_i)^2$. All intermediate results computed by parallel workers are then reduced by applying a sum operator. The final result is then divided by the total number of tuples as defined by the mathematical definition $$MSE = \frac{1}{n}\sum_{i=1}^{n}(v_i - p_i)^2$$. Note that Spark hides all the low level details to the programmer by allowing to write a distributed code which is very close to a mathematical formulation. The code adopts python lambda computation for compact representations of anonymous functions.

Code

```
MSE = valuesAndPreds.map(lambda (v, p): (v - p)**2).reduce(lambda x, y: x +
y) / valuesAndPreds.count()
```

Spark can however support additional forms of parallel computation by taking inspiration from the 20 years of work on skeletons computations and, more recently, on Microsoft's Cosmos.[9]

11. Can you provide examples for other computations in Spark?

Solution

The first code fragment is an example of map reduction, where we want to find the line with most words in a text. First each line is mapped into the number of words it contains. Then those numbers are reduced and the maximum is taken. Pretty simple: one single line of code stays here for something which requires hundreds of lines in other parallel paradigms such as Hadoop.

Spark supports two types of operations: *transformations*, which create a new RDD dataset from an existing one, and *actions*, which return a value to the driver program after running a computation on the dataset. All transformations in Spark are lazy because the computation is postponed as much as possible until the results are really needed by the program. This allows Spark to run efficiently – for example the compiler can realize that an RDD created through *map* will be used in a *reduce* and return only the result of the *reduce* to the driver, rather than the larger mapped dataset. Intermediate results can be persisted and cached.

Basic transformations include (the list below is not comprehensive. Check online for a full list[10])

Transformation	Use
map(func)	Returns a new distributed dataset formed by passing each element of the source through a function func.
filter(func)	Returns a new dataset formed by selecting those elements of the source on which func returns true.

[9] http://codingplayground.blogspot.co.at/2010/09/cosmos-massive-computation-in-microsoft.html

[10]http://spark.apache.org/docs/latest/programming-guide.html#transformations

flatMap(func)	Similar to map, but each input item can be mapped to 0 or more output items (so func should return a Seq rather than a single item).
sample(withReplacement, fraction, seed)	Samples a fraction of the data, with or without replacement, using a given random number generator seed.
union(otherDataset)	Returns a new dataset that contains the union of the elements in the source dataset and argument.
intersection(otherDataset)	Returns a new RDD that contains the intersection of elements in the source dataset and argument.
distinct([numTasks]))	Returns a new dataset that contains the distinct elements of the source dataset.
groupByKey([numTasks])	When called on a dataset of (K, V) pairs, a dataset of (K, Iterable<V>) pairs returns.
reduceByKey(func, [numTasks])	When called on a dataset of (K, V) pairs, a dataset of (K, V) pairs returns, where the values for each key are aggregated using the given reduce function func, which must be of type (V,V) => V
sortByKey([ascending], [numTasks])	When called on a dataset of (K, V) pairs, where K implements Ordered, a dataset of (K, V) pairs sorted by keys in ascending or descending order returns, as specified in the boolean ascending argument.

join(otherDataset, [numTasks])	When called on datasets of type (K, V) and (K, W), a dataset of (K, (V, W)) pairs with all pairs of elements for each key returns. Outer joins are here supported throughleftOuterJoin, rightOuterJoin, andfullOuterJoin.

Basic actions include (the list below is not comprehensive. Check it online for a full list[11])

Actions	Use
reduce(func)	Aggregates the elements of the dataset using a function func (which takes two arguments and returns one). The function should be commutative and associative so that it can be computed correctly in parallel.
collect()	Returns all the elements of the dataset as an array at the driver program. This is usually useful after a filter or other operations that return a sufficiently small subset of data.
count()	Returns the number of elements in the dataset.
take(n)	Returns an array with the first n elements of the

---

[11]http://spark.apache.org/docs/latest/programming-guide.html#transformations

	dataset.
takeSample(withReplacement,num, [seed])	Returns an array with a random sample of numelements of the dataset, with or without replacement, optionally pre-specifying a random number generator seed.
countByKey()	Only available on RDDs of type (K, V). A hashmap of (K, Int) pairs with the count of each key returns.
foreach(func)	Runs a function func on each element of the dataset. This is usually done for side effects such as updating an Accumulator or interacting with external storage systems.

Spark supports also two special types of variables. **Broadcasts**, that allow the programmer to keep a read-only variable cached on each machine, and **Accumulators** for efficient implementation of counters.

The second code fragment is another map reduction, where the text is transformed into a flatmap of words. Words are then mapped into number 1 because we count each occurrence as pairs (words, 1). Then a reduceByKey() operation allows to aggregate each word and sum the occurrences. Again pretty simple: one single line in Spark using a functional programming style. The third code segment introduces accumulators and broadcast variables.

Code

```
# map reduce
textFile.map(lambda line: len(line.split())).reduce(lambda a, b: a if (a > b) else b)

# word count
```

```
wordCounts = textFile.flatMap(lambda line: line.split()).map(lambda word:
(word, 1)).reduceByKey(lambda a, b: a+b)

# broadcast
broadcastVar = sc.broadcast([1, 2, 3])

# accumulators
accum = sc.accumulator(0)
sc.parallelize([1, 2, 3, 4]).foreach(lambda x: accum.add(x))
```

12. How does Python interact with Spark

Solution

Spark has a dedicate API for Python called PySpark exposing access to the
Spark programming framework. Internally Spark has been developed using
Scala, a functional programming language which integrates well with JVM,
the java virtual machine. One important observation is that Python is
dynamically typed, so RDDs can hold objects of multiple types. Another
observation is that the PySpark APIs reflect the Scala APIs but the former
typically take a Python function and return a Python collection. Also lambda
functions are supported and used quite frequently.

Functions used for transformations are sent to the workers for code
execution together with serialized data and instances of classes. Python also
supports an interactive shell `./bin/pyspark` for performing Data science at
the command line.

It is important to point out that Spark compilers allocate the computation on
the underlying network of servers with no explicit need of dealing with low
level details for programmers, unless this is explicitly desired.

13. What is Spark support for Machine Learning?

Solution

Spark has a powerful library called MLIB for Machine learning. Mlib supports
computation of Basic Statistics and Features extraction, selection and
transformation. It also supports Classification and Regression with linear
models, naïve Bayes, decision trees and ensembles. Plus, Mlib implements
Collaborative Filtering, Clustering with k-means, Gaussian, LDA, Associative

Rule mining and Dimensional Reduction. Many optimization problems are solved by using the Distributed Stochastic Gradient Descent. We will discuss all these techniques in this volume and in the next one.

14.How does Spark work in a parallel environment

Solution

Spark adopts a simple model for parallel computation. A driver program interacts with the worker nodes by using the SparkContext environment variable. This interaction is transparent to the user. Each worker node executes assigned tasks and can cache locally the results for computation for future reuse. The results of computations are sent back to the driver program.

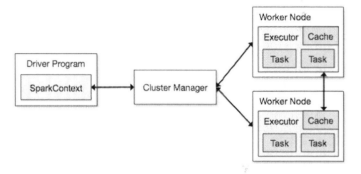

Code

```
conf = SparkConf().setAppName(appName).setMaster(master)
sc = SparkContext(conf=conf)
```

15.What is the mean, the variance, and the covariance?

Solution

In arithmetic terms the *mean,* or *mathematical expectation,* is the central value of a discrete set of numbers X, which is the so-called random variable, the value of which is subjected to variations due to chance. The mean is defined as the sum of values divided by the number of n values:

$$E[X] = \mu(X) = \frac{x_1 + \ldots + x_n}{n} = \frac{1}{n}\sum_{i=1}^{n} x_i$$

The *variance* measures how far a set of numbers is spread out. A variance of zero shows that all the values are equal; a small variance indicates that the data points tend to be very close to the mean and therefore to each other, while a high variance indicates that the data points are more spread out. Variance is always positive. Given a random variable X the variance is defined as

$$VAR(X) = \sigma(X) = E\big[(X - E[X])^2\big]$$

The *covariance* is a measure of how much two random variables change together. Mathematically:

$$COV(X, Y) = \sigma(X, Y) = E[(X - E[X])(Y - E[Y])]$$

Code

```
import numpy as np
x = np.array([[0, 2], [1, 1], [2, 0]]).T
print np.mean(x[1,])
print np.var(x[1,])
print np.cov(x)
```

1.0
0.666666666667
[[1. -1.]
 [-1. 1.]]

16.What are percentiles and quartiles?

Solution

A percentile is a metric indicating a value, below which a given percentage of observations falls. For instance: the 50th percentile is the median of a vector of observations; the 25th percentile is the first quartile, the 50th percentile is the second and the 75th percentile is the third one. When the time to provide a service is considered, the 90th, the 95th and the 99th percentiles are generally reported. Percentiles are more resilient than mathematical averages to the contribution of the so-called outliers, e.g. data points that are significantly spread out by the majority of the observations.

```
import numpy as np
x = np.array([0, 1, 4, 5, 6, 8, 8, 9, 11, 10, 19, 19.2, 19.7, 3])
for i in [75, 90, 95, 99]:
    print i, np.percentile(x, i)
```

17. Can you transform an XML file into Python Pandas?

This is a question about data transformation. XML is commonly used for representing structured information. For instance this could be an XML fragment for representing books data:

```
<?xml version="1.0"?>
<catalog>
  <book id="bk101">
    <author>Gambardella, Matthew</author>
    <title>XML Developer's Guide</title>
    <genre>Computer</genre>
    <price>44.95</price>
    <publish_date>2000-10-01</publish_date>
    <description>An in-depth look at creating applications
    with XML.</description>
  </book>
...
</catalog>
```

Pandas are a powerful set of Python libraries for data analysis. One key data structure in Pandas is the DataFrame, which is a Two-dimensional size-mutable, potentially heterogeneous tabular data structure with labeled axes (rows and columns). Each row is called a Series.

Pandas offer a rich set of APIs for manipulating DataFrames. In this code example an XML file is read using the convenient objectify module and a Pandas data structure is then created accordingly.

```
from lxml import objectify
```

```python
import pandas as pd

# open and parse xml
xml = objectify.parse(open('book.xml'))
root = xml.getroot()

# pandas and dataframes
df = pd.DataFrame(columns=('Author', 'Title', 'Genre'))

for i in range(0, 10):
    row = dict(zip(['Author', 'Title', 'Genre'],
    [root.book[i].author, root.book[i].title,
    root.book[i].genre
    ]))
    rowSeries = pd.Series(row)
    rowSeries.name = i
    df = df.append(rowSeries)

print df
```

```
                    Author                        Title \
0  [[[Gambardella, Matthew]]]          [[[XML Developer's Guide]]]
1       [[[Ralls, Kim]]]              [[[Midnight Rain]]]
2       [[[Corets, Eva]]]             [[[Maeve Ascendant]]]
3       [[[Corets, Eva]]]             [[[Oberon's Legacy]]]
4       [[[Corets, Eva]]]            [[[The Sundered Grail]]]
5    [[[Randall, Cynthia]]]            [[[Lover Birds]]]
6    [[[Thurman, Paula]]]             [[[Splish Splash]]]
7    [[[Knorr, Stefan]]]             [[[Creepy Crawlies]]]
8    [[[Kress, Peter]]]               [[[Paradox Lost]]]
9    [[[O'Brien, Tim]]] [[[Microsoft .NET: The Programming Bible]]]

               Genre
0      [[[Computer]]]
1      [[[Fantasy]]]
2      [[[Fantasy]]]
3      [[[Fantasy]]]
4      [[[Fantasy]]]
5      [[[Romance]]]
6      [[[Romance]]]
7       [[[Horror]]]
8 [[[Science Fiction]]]
9      [[[Computer]]]
```

18.Can you read HTML into Python Pandas?

Solution

Another question about accessing data. Python Pandas are also convenient for working with HMTL files downloaded from the network. This small code fragment is all we need to download some HTML data, parse it and load it into a suitable DataFrame.

Code

```
import pandas as pd
url = 'http://www.fdic.gov/bank/individual/failed/banklist.html'
dfs = pd.read_html(url)
print dfs
```

[		Bank Name	City	ST \
0	Premier Bank	Denver	CO
1	Edgebrook Bank	Chicago	IL
2	Doral BankEn Espanol	San Juan	PR
3	Capitol City Bank & Trust Company	Atlanta	GA
4	Highland Community Bank	Chicago	IL
5	First National Bank of Crestview	Crestview	FL

19.Can you read JSON into Python Pandas?

Solution

Json is a compact representation of structured data. This simple code snippet loads data from the network and transforms it into Pandas data structure.

Code

```
from urllib2 import Request, urlopen
import json
import pandas as pd
from pandas.io.json import json_normalize
path1 = '42.974049,-81.205203|42.974298,-81.195755'
request=Request('http://maps.googleapis.com/maps/api/elevation/json?locations='
+path1+'&sensor=false')
response = urlopen(request)
elevations = response.read()
data = pd.read_json(elevations)
print json_normalize(data['results'])
```

elevation location.lat location.lng resolution

0 243.346268   42.974049   -81.205203   19.087904

20. Can you draw a function from Python?

Solution

Visualizing data is key for any machine learning activity and a good Data Scientist knows how to use data visualization tools. For instance Matplotlib is a convenient plotting tool in Python. The following code snippet shows how to plot a function.

Code

```
import matplotlib.pyplot as plt
import numpy as np
from scipy.special import expit
x = np.arange(-10., 10., 0.2)
sig = expit(x)
plt.plot(x,sig)
plt.show()
```

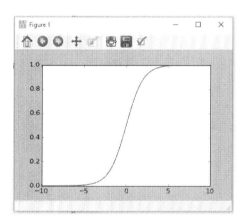

21. Can you represent a graph in Python?

Solution

Python provides a convenient library for graph representation named Networkx[12] , which provides support for direct / indirect graphs and multigraphs. Also many graph algorithms are already implemented in the framework. This simple code snippet computes the connected components algorithm.

Code

```
import networkx as nx

G=nx.Graph()
#add nodes (1,2,3) and edges(1,2), (1,3)
G.add_edges_from([(1,2),(1,3)])
c = nx.connected_components(G)
```

22. What is an Ipython notebook?

Solution

Ipython notebook is a convenient interface for executing Python codes directly from a web browser. The following command starts the environment and the browser:

ipython notebook
[I   21:17:06.706   NotebookApp]   Using   MathJax   from   CDN: https://cdn.mathjax.org/mathjax/latest/MathJax.js
[I   21:17:07.252   NotebookApp]   Serving   notebooks   from   local   directory: C:\Users\agull_000\Dropbox\python
[I 21:17:07.252 NotebookApp] 0 active kernels
[I 21:17:07.252 NotebookApp] The IPython Notebook is running at: http://localhost:8888/
[I 21:17:07.252 NotebookApp] Use Control-C to stop this server and shut down all kernels (twice to skip confirmation).
[I 21:17:21.631 NotebookApp] Creating new notebook in
[I 21:17:30.592 NotebookApp] Kernel started: 50260c3a-e7cc-426f-84fa-9ea630886103

Code

This code fragment prints few circles and it is executed directly from the browser.

---

[12] https://networkx.github.io/documentation/latest/tutorial/tutorial.html

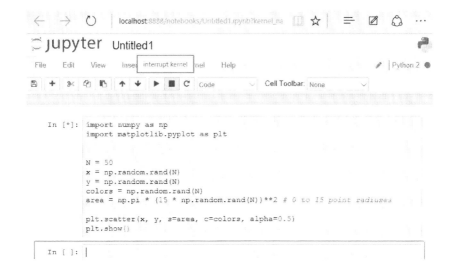

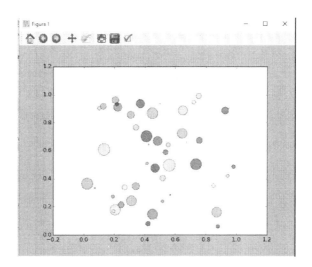

23.What is a convenient tool for performing data statistics?

Solution

Pandas provide a nice framework for data-analysis. In this code example an *iris* toy dataset is loaded and then the mean, the standard deviation and different percentiles are computed.

Code

```
import pandas as pd
import numpy as np
from sklearn.datasets import load_iris
iris = load_iris()

irisNP = iris.data
irisDF = pd.DataFrame(iris.data, columns=iris.feature_names)

# group by target category
irisDF['group'] = pd.Series([iris.target_names[k] for k in iris.target],
dtype='category')

#mean, std, quantile
print irisDF.mean(numeric_only=True)
print irisDF.std()
print irisDF.quantile(np.array([0, .25, 0.50, .75, .90, .99]))
```

sepal length (cm)	5.843333
sepal width (cm)	3.054000
petal length (cm)	3.758667
petal width (cm)	1.198667
sepal length (cm)	0.828066
sepal width (cm)	0.433594
petal length (cm)	1.764420
petal width (cm)	0.763161

	sepal length (cm)	sepal width (cm)	petal length (cm)	petal width (cm)
0.00	4.3	2.000	1.00	0.1
0.25	5.1	2.800	1.60	0.3
0.50	5.8	3.000	4.35	1.3
0.75	6.4	3.300	5.10	1.8
0.90	6.9	3.610	5.80	2.2
0.99	7.7	4.151	6.70	2.5

24.How is it convenient to visualize data statistics

Solution

Pandas provide support for a boxplot visualization, a convenient way of graphically representing groups of numerical values through their quartiles. Boxplots may also have vertically extending lines from the boxes indicating variability outside the upper and lower quartiles. Outliers may be plotted as individual points. In this example of code we have represented a set of trials of 10 observations of a uniform random variable on $[0,1)$.

Code

```
import pandas as pd
import numpy as np
import matplotlib
import matplotlib.pyplot as plt

df = pd.DataFrame(np.random.rand(10, 5), columns=['A', 'B', 'C', 'D', 'E'])
df.plot(kind='box')
plt.show()
```

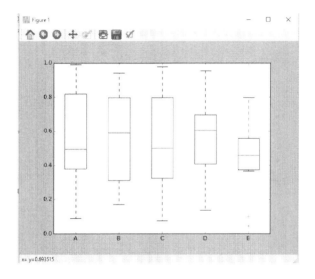

25.How to compute covariance and correlation matrices with pandas

Solution

Pandas provides support for covariance computation. This simple code snippet computes covariance and correlation for an iris toy dataset. Remember that correlation is equivalent to computing covariance on standardized random variables. For instance it can be observed that sepal length is positively correlated with petal length.

Code

```
import pandas as pd
import numpy as np
from sklearn.datasets import load_iris
iris = load_iris()

irisNP = iris.data
irisDF = pd.DataFrame(iris.data, columns=iris.feature_names)

# group by target category
irisDF['group'] = pd.Series([iris.target_names[k] for k in iris.target],
dtype='category')

print irisDF.cov()
print irisDF.corr()
```

	sepal length (cm)	sepal width (cm)	petal length (cm) \
sepal length (cm)	0.685694	-0.039268	1.273682
sepal width (cm)	-0.039268	0.188004	-0.321713
petal length (cm)	1.273682	-0.321713	3.113179
petal width (cm)	0.516904	-0.117981	1.296387

	petal width (cm)
sepal length (cm)	0.516904
sepal width (cm)	-0.117981
petal length (cm)	1.296387
petal width (cm)	0.582414

	sepal length (cm)	sepal width (cm)	petal length (cm) \
sepal length (cm)	1.000000	-0.109369	0.871754
sepal width (cm)	-0.109369	1.000000	-0.420516
petal length (cm)	0.871754	-0.420516	1.000000
petal width (cm)	0.817954	-0.356544	0.962757

	petal width (cm)
sepal length (cm)	0.817954
sepal width (cm)	-0.356544
petal length (cm)	0.962757
petal width (cm)	1.000000

26.Can you provide an example of connection to the Twitter API?

Solution

Twitter provides a convenient API for accessing data. The first step is to register within the site at https://apps.twitter.com/app/new and require a *Consumer Key, a Consumer Secret,* an *Access Key* and an *Access Secret.* Then this code fragment can be used for accessing the live stream of twitter trends.

Code

```
import tweepy, json

CONSUMER_KEY = 'mX-------------------------------'
CONSUMER_SECRET = '-----------------------------------
------'

ACCESS_KEY = '-----------------------------------------------'
ACCESS_SECRET = '--------------------------------------'
auth = tweepy.OAuthHandler(CONSUMER_KEY, CONSUMER_SECRET)
auth.set_access_token(ACCESS_KEY, ACCESS_SECRET)
api = tweepy.API(auth)

trends1 = api.trends_place(1)
print trends1
```

[{u'created_at': u'2015-09-08T09:33:39Z', u'trends': [{u'url': u'http://twitter.com/search?q=%23Vatan%C4%B1mU%C4%9Fruna', u'query': u'%23Vatan%C4%B1mU%C4%9Fruna', u'name': u'#Vatan\u0131mU\u011fruna', u'promoted_content': None}, {u'url': u'http://twitter.com/searc h?q=%23I%C4%9Fd%C4%B1r', u'query': u'%23I%C4%9Fd%C4%B1r', u'name': u'#I\u011fd\u0131r', u'promoted_content': None}, {u'url': u'http: //twitter.com/search?q=%23%D9%85%D8%A7%D8%B0%D8%A7_%D8%A7%D8%B3%D8% AA%D9%81%D8%AF%D9%86%D8%A7_%D9%85%D9%86_%D8%B3%D9%86%D8%A7%D8 %A8_ %D8%B4%D8%A7%D8%AA', u'query': u'%23%D9%85%D8%A7%D8%B0%D8%A7_%D8%A7%D8%B3%D8%AA%D9%81%D8%AF%D 9%86%D8%A7_%D9%85%D9%86_%D8%B3%D9%86%D8 %A7%D8%A8_%D8%B4%D8%A7%D8%AA', u'name': u'#\u0645\u0627\u0630\u0627_\u0627\u0633\u062a\u0641\u062f\u0646\u0627_\u064 5\u0646_\u0633\u u0646\u0627\u0628_\u0634\u0627\u062a', u'promoted_content': None}, {u'url': u'http://twitter.com/search?q=%EB%92%B7%EB%8B%B4%ED%99%94

', u'query': u'%EB%92%B7%EB%8B%B4%ED%99%94', u'name': u'\ub4b7\ub2f4\ud654', u'promoted_content': None}, {u'url': u'http://twitter.c
om/search?q=%23FelizMartes', u'query': u'%23FelizMartes', u'name': u'#FelizMartes', u'promoted_content': None}, {u'url': u'http://tw
itter.com/search?q=%23%D8%AA%D8%A7%D9%88%D8%B1_%D8%AC%D8%AF%D9%8A%
D8%AF_%D8%A8%D8%A7%D9%84%D8%B3%D8%B9%D9%88%D8%AF%D9%8A%D9%87',
u'q
uery':
u'%23%D8%AA%D8%A7%D9%88%D8%B1_%D8%AC%D8%AF%D9%8A%D8%AF_%D8%A8%
D8%A7%D9%84%D8%B3%D8%B9%D9%88%D8%AF%D9%8A%D9%87', u'name': u'#\
u062a\u0627\u0648\u0631_\u062c\u062f\u064a\u062f_\u0628\u0627\u0644\u0633\u0
639\u0648\u062f\u064a\u0647', u'promoted_content': None}
, {u'url': u'http://twitter.com/search?q=%22Sam+Smith%22', u'query':
u'%22Sam+Smith%22', u'name': u'Sam Smith', u'promoted_content':
None}, {u'url': u'http://twitter.com/search?q=%22Felices+140%22', u'query':
u'%22Felices+140%22', u'name': u'Felices 140', u'promot
ed_content': None}, {u'url':
u'http://twitter.com/search?q=%22%EC%B2%9C%EC%82%AC%EC%99%80+%EC%95%85%
EB%A7%88%22', u'query': u'%22%EC
%B2%9C%EC%82%AC%EC%99%80+%EC%95%85%EB%A7%88%22', u'name':
u'\ucc9c\uc0ac\uc640 \uc545\ub9c8', u'promoted_content': None}, {u'url': u
'http://twitter.com/search?q=%22Alexander+Pacteau%22', u'query':
u'%22Alexander+Pacteau%22', u'name': u'Alexander Pacteau', u'promot
ed_content': None}], u'as_of': u'2015-09-08T09:37:06Z', u'locations': [{u'woeid': 1,
u'name': u'Worldwide'}]}]

27. Can you provide an example of connection to the LinkedIn API?

Solution

Linkedin has an API for accessing the content. First, the application should be registered within the site on https://www.linkedin.com/developer/apps/ for getting the API_KEY and the API_SECRET. It is also important to register the correct RETURN_URL. The authentication.authorization_url should be then opened in a browser for letting the user logging in via OAUTH standard protocol[13]. The returned code can be used as authentication.authorization_code for getting access.

Code

from linkedin import linkedin

---

[13] http://oauth.net/2/

```
API_KEY = '--------'
API_SECRET = '---'
RETURN_URL = 'http://localhost:8000'

authentication = linkedin.LinkedInAuthentication(API_KEY, API_SECRET,
RETURN_URL, linkedin.PERMISSIONS.enums.values())
print authentication.authorization_url  # open this url on your browser
application = linkedin.LinkedInApplication(authentication)
authentication.authorization_code = '--------------------------------'
authentication.get_access_token()
connections = application.get_connections()
print connections
```

28.Can you provide an example of connection to the Facebook API?

Solution

Facebook has a nice API accessible on https://developers.facebook.com/docs/graph-api/overview and the following code fragment provides basic usage for getting friends' connections with the user's profile and for posting them on the Facebook wall.

Code

```
import facebook

# how to get the access token https://developers.facebook.com/docs/graph-api/overview
graph = facebook.GraphAPI(oauth_access_token)
profile = graph.get_object("me")
friends = graph.get_connections("me", "friends")
graph.put_object("me", "feed", message="Posting in my wall")
```

29.What is a TFxIDF?

Solution

TFxIDF is a weighting technique frequently used for text classifications. The key intuition is to boost a term t which is frequent for a document $d \in D$ in a collection of documents D (Term Frequency=TF) but t is not so frequent in all

the remaining documents in D (Inverse Document Frequency, IDF).
Mathematically

- $TF(t,d)$ is the number of times for term t to appear in document d
- $DF(t,D)$ is the number of documents containing term t
- $$IDF(t,D) = log\frac{|D| + 1}{DF(t,D) + 1}$$

Note that $IDF(t, D)$ is zero, if a term appears in all the documents. Also note that a smoothing factor of one has been used if a term does not appear in a document for avoiding a division by zero. Spark implements TFxIDF by hashing the words into a more compact representation which avoids global and expensive terms-to-index mapping, involving all the words in the collection regardless of the server where the data has been partitioned.

Code

```
from pyspark import SparkContext
from pyspark.mllib.feature import HashingTF
from pyspark.mllib.feature import IDF
sc = SparkContext()

# Load documents (one per line).
documents = sc.textFile("...").map(lambda line: line.split(" "))

#hash the terms and compute the TF on documents
hashingTF = HashingTF()
tf = hashingTF.transform(documents)

# force the real computation
tf.cache()

# compute the global IDF: ignore too rare terms < 2 documents
idf = IDF(minDocFreq=2).fit(tf)

# do the TFxIDF in a distributed fashion
tfidf = idf.transform(tf)
```

30. What is "features hashing"? And why is it useful for BigData?

Solution

If the space of features is high dimensional, one way to reduce dimensionality is via hashing. For instance: we might combine two discrete but sparse features into one and only denser discrete synthetically created feature by transforming the original observations. This transformation introduces an error because it suffers from potential hash collisions, since different raw features may become the same term after hashing.

However this model might be more compact and, in some situations, we might decide to trade off this risk either for simplicity or because this is the only viable option to handle very large datasets (Big Data).

More sophisticate forms of hashing such as Bloom Filters[14], Count Min-Sketches[15], minHash[16] and Local Sensitive Hashing[17] are more advanced techniques which will be discussed in the next volume.

31. What is "continuous features binning"?

Solution

If a feature assumes continuous values then it could be convenient to discretize it via hashing or binning. This intuition is very simple: the space of continuous values is divided into buckets, in which the first ones are hashed.

32. What is an L^P normalization?

Solution

Features might be transformed in such a way that they have unit norm L^P, where L^P can be either norm-1, or norm-2, or norm-∞

---

[14] https://en.wikipedia.org/wiki/Bloom_filter
[15] https://en.wikipedia.org/wiki/Count%E2%80%93min_sketch
[16] https://en.wikipedia.org/wiki/MinHash
[17] https://en.wikipedia.org/wiki/Locality-sensitive_hashing

Code

```
from pyspark.mllib.util import MLUtils
from pyspark.mllib.linalg import Vectors
from pyspark.mllib.feature import Normalizer

data = MLUtils.loadLibSVMFile(sc, "data/mllib/sample_libsvm_data.txt")
labels = data.map(lambda x: x.label)
features = data.map(lambda x: x.features)

normalizer1 = Normalizer()

# scale every feature normalizing with norm-2
data1 = labels.zip(normalizer1.transform(features))
```

33. What is a Chi Square Selection?

Solution

Chi-Square is a statistical test used to understand if two categorical features are correlated. In this case it might be useful to discard one of them in order to keep the model simpler. This method works by ordering features based on a Chi-Squared test of independence from the class, and then by filtering all top features, which are most closely related to the label. Suppose that an event has expected frequencies of observations e_i and observed frequencies o_i, then the Chi Square test is

$$\chi^2 = \sum_{i=1}^{K} \frac{(e_i - o_i)^2}{e_i}$$

Spark supports Chi-Square tests for feature selection since version 1.4.0

34. What is mutual information and how can it be used for features selection?

Solution

Recalling that information entropy is $H(X) = \sum_{i=1}^{n} p(X_i) log\, p(X_i)$, where X is a random variable, mutual information computes how much two features have in common. This is defined as

$$I(X,Y) = \sum_{i=1}^{m}\sum_{j=1}^{n} p(X_i, Y_j) log\, p(X_i, Y_j)$$

The normalized mutual information is in interval $[0,1]$ defined as

$$NI(X, Y) = \frac{I(X,Y)}{H(X) + H(Y)}$$

Computing mutual information in Spark is left as an exercise.

35. What is a loss function, what are linear models, and what do we mean by regularization parameters in machine learning?

Solution

A loss function maps a set of observed events represented by one or more variables onto a real number, which represents the associated "cost". Machine learning frequently deals with modelling the observed data by minimizing the costs of a suitable loss function. In particular given an algorithmic prediction p and a true label y from a gold set, a loss function $L(p, y)$ measures the difference between p and y.

An important class of machine learning methods is the one of linear methods, where the task is to minimize a convex function f on a variable vector w with k real entries ($w \in R^k$).

It should be noticed that if function f is convex and has a derivative, then f will have a unique minimum and this minimum can be analytically derived[18].

This minimization task error can be formally expressed as $\min_{w \in R^k} f(w)$ where the objective function f has the following form:

$$f(w) = \lambda R(w) + \frac{1}{n} \sum_{i=1}^{n} L(w; x_i, y)$$

where $x_i \in R^k \; i = 1,..n$ are the training examples, y is the vector of true labels and $w \in R^k$ is a set of weights which are algorithmically computed in such a way that the error of the model learned from the training data x is minimized. This error is expressed by a well-chosen loss function $L(w; x_i, y)$ (see next question for few examples).

This method is called "linear" because prediction p is a linear combination of w and x, computed with a simple vector multiplication $p = w^T x$, and $L(w; x_i, y)$ is a function of p and y.

The factor $R(w)$ is introduced also to control the complexity of this model. In turn the regularization hyper-parameter $\lambda \geq 0$ balances the trade-off between the goal of minimizing the loss function and the goal of minimizing the model complexity. For instance, it could be sometimes better to have a slightly more expensive model in terms of loss function costs, if the model is simpler from the point of view of sparsity of weights (number of zero entries in w).

The two tables below contain a summary of the most common used loss functions and regularization factors for linear methods:

Name	Loss Function	Derivative	Labels	Meaning	Example

---

[18] https://en.wikipedia.org/wiki/Convex_function

	Loss	Derivative	Label	Description	Use case
Squared	$\frac{1}{2}(w^T x - y)^2$	$(w^T x - y)x$	Real, $y \in R$	It expresses the squared distance between the prediction and the true label	Linear regression, for example expected return on stock investment
Logistic	$l = log(1 + e^{-yw^T x})$	$-y\left(1 - \frac{1}{l}\right)x$	Positive / Negative, $y \in \{-1,1\}$	It is used to predict a binary response	Logistic regression, for example expected click on search ads
Hinge	$\max\{0, 1 - yw^T x\}$	$\begin{cases} -yx & yw^T x < 1 \\ 0 & ow \end{cases}$	Positive / Negative, $y \in \{-1,1\}$	It is used for classification	SVM, for example image recognition

This is a typical plot for squared, logistic and hinge loss functions

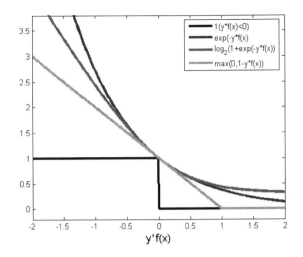

This is a summary of the most commonly used regularization factors.

Name	R(W)	Derivative	Meaning
L1	$\|\|w\|\|_1 = \sum_{i=1}^{n} \|x_i\|$	$sign(w)$	norm-1 for vectors
L2	$\frac{1}{2}\|\|w\|\|_2^2 = \frac{1}{2}\sum_{i=1}^{n} x_i^2$	w	squared norm-2 for vectors

36. What is an odd ratio?

Solution

Given a probability p the odd ratio simply identifies the chances for the event to happen over the chances for the event not to happen. The event $\frac{p}{1-p}$ is a function $[0,1] \rightarrow [0,\infty)$. If we take the logarithm, we have $\log\left(\frac{p}{1-p}\right)$ and we can thus map the range of probabilities [0, 1] into the full range $(-\infty, +\infty)$.

The concept of "odd ratio" is also useful to introduce "logistic regression" (the topic of the next question). Let us assume that we have a linear equation $y_i = a + bx_i$, we can imagine that y_i is represented in terms of log odds so that $\log\left(\dfrac{p}{1-p}\right) = a + bx_i$ which can be solved for p_i as $p_i = \dfrac{1}{1 + e^{-(a+bx_i)}}$

and the problem becomes the one of finding the lowest error for all training examples (x_i, p_i)

37.What is a sigmoid function and what is a logistic function?

Solution

A sigmoid function has the following mathematical formulation $\sigma{:}R{\rightarrow}[0,1]$

$$\sigma(h) = \frac{1}{1 + e^{-h}}$$

Sigmoid functions are used frequently in machine learning in particular in neural networks. Their name is related to the typical "S" shape when plotted. Note that for input in $(-\infty,\infty)$ the output is in [0, 1], so the sigmoid is useful to map real values into probabilities.

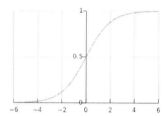

One important property is that the first order derivative of a sigmoid has a very simple formula

$$\frac{\partial}{\partial h}\sigma(h) = \frac{\partial}{\partial h}(1 + e^{-h})^{-1} = -1(1 + e^{-h})^{-2}\frac{\partial}{\partial h}(1 + e^{-h}) =$$

$$-1(1 + e^{-h})^{-2}(-e^{-h}) = \frac{e^{-h}}{(1 + e^{-h})^2} = \frac{1}{(1 + e^{-h})}\frac{e^{-h}}{(1 + e^{-h})} =$$

$\sigma(h)(1 - \sigma(h))$

A logistic function is a particular type of sigmoid function used in linear regression $f(x) = \dfrac{M}{1 + e^{-\beta(h - h_0)}}$, where M is the maximum value, β is the steepness of the curve and h_0 is the x-value of the sigmoid midpoint.

Code

```
from scipy.special import expit
expit(0.467)
```

Note that in a previous question we already plotted a sigmoid.

38. What is a gradient descent?

Solution

Mathematically the gradient ∇f of a function f is a vector, the components of which are the n partial derivatives of f. Similarly to the derivative, the gradient represents the slope of the function graph tangent and therefore the gradient points in the direction of the greatest rate of the function increase rate, while its magnitude is the slope of the graph in that direction. As a consequence $-\nabla f$ points to the direction of a function maximum decrease rate.

In many Supervised Machine Learning problems, we need to learn a model by using a training dataset. A popular and easy-to-use technique to estimate the model parameters is to minimize the error associated to the model by using the appropriate Gradient Descent technique. The Gradient Descent iteratively estimates the weights by moving in the direction which minimizes a chosen cost function at every step.

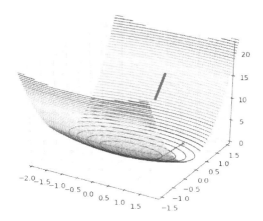

The pseudo-code is here very simple. Until either some convergence or termination criteria is met, the weights of the model are updated according the following rule

$$w_{i+1} = w_i - \lambda \frac{\nabla f}{\nabla w}$$

where $\frac{\nabla f}{\nabla w}$ is the gradient in w and λ is a learning rate parameter.

If the function is convex, then the gradient descend will find a unique minimum, otherwise the technique can be trapped into a local minimum or it might incur into the risk of not converging. Therefore, it is mandatory to stop iterations if a chosen maximum number of iteration is reached. In addition to that, it could be useful to repeat the process for different initial values w_0 in order to detect if the process is trapped in a local minimum.

The learning rate parameter λ determines how fast or slow we will move towards the optimal solution. If λ is very large, the optimal solution will be skipped. If it is too small, we will need many iterations to converge to the best values. One possible solution is to scale λ according to how close the solution is. In other words: λ could be scaled according to the error rate measured in each iteration.

39.What is a stochastic gradient descent?

Solution

Many machine learning problems can be formulated as minimization problems of an objective function, which is the sum of many functions f_i , each one associated to the i-th observation in the training set:

$$min_w F(w) \text{ where } F(w) = \sum_{i=1}^{n} f_i(w)$$

The gradient $\nabla F(w)$ can be computationally very expensive because at each iteration all dataset observations should be taken into account and the standard update rule would be

$$w_{i+1} = w_i - \lambda \frac{\nabla F(w)}{\nabla w} = w_i - \lambda \sum_{i=1}^{n} \frac{\nabla f_i(w)}{\nabla w}$$

One solution is to sample a subset of summand functions at every step. This approach is called "stochastic gradient descent" and it is very effective in the case of large-scale machine learning problems. One simple variant of stochastic gradient descent is to consider one training example at time and update only that gradient component. Another more sophisticated approach is called "mini-batches" which computes the gradient against more than one training example at each step. This can be a vectorial operation which is very efficient for modern computers.

Code

In Spark the sampling of training examples is performed using RDD distributed datasets, while the computation of the partial results sum is performed by using local working machines which then update a master server.[19] The following is an abstract from Spark API

---

[19]https://spark.apache.org/docs/latest/api/scala/index.html#org.apache.spark.mllib.optimization.GradientDescent

```
def optimize(data: RDD[(Double, Vector)], Developer API
    initialWeights: Vector): Vector
```
Runs gradient descent on the given training data.

```
def setGradient(gradient: Gradient):
    GradientDescent.this.type
```
Set the gradient function (of the loss function of one single data example) to be used for SGD.

```
def setMiniBatchFraction(fraction:         Experimental
    Double): GradientDescent.this.type
```
Set fraction of data to be used for each SGD iteration.

```
def setNumIterations(iters: Int):
    GradientDescent.this.type
```
Set the number of iterations for SGD.

```
def setRegParam(regParam: Double):
    GradientDescent.this.type
```
Set the regularization parameter.

```
def setStepSize(step: Double):
    GradientDescent.this.type
```
Set the initial step size of SGD for the first step.

```
def setUpdater(updater: Updater):
    GradientDescent.this.type
```
Set the updater function to actually perform a gradient step in a given direction.

40. What is a Linear Least Square Regression?

Solution

Linear models are simple and provide data partition based on straight lines. In general, they require a reasonably small amount of training data. More complex models, such as SVM with kernels and ensembles (which will be introduced in the next volume), allow data separation with more sophisticate curves - not only with straight lines - but they are in general more expensive to train, require more data, and are also more expensive when they predict results on unseen data.

In many real applications linear models with regularizations are instead providing good performances and are extremely fast for training or when deployed. Also linear models show a very nice characteristic for they allow to easily understand the importance of each feature. This is called "variable importance information" and it consists in ranking each selected feature: a highly ranked feature contributes more to reduce the error for a model than a low ranked feature. So this ranking operation can guide Data scientists to pick the right set of features by discarding some of them and by adding others. Note that a linear model with regularization provides sparse solutions for learning.

When new unseen data is applied the forecast can therefore be computed with very simple operations consisting in few sums and few multiplications.

As discussed, Regression is the task of forecasting a numeric value. Linear Regression is a method of finding $\min_{w \in R^k} f(w)$ where the objective function is a loss function

$$f(w) = \lambda R(w) + \frac{1}{n} \sum_{1=1}^{n} L(w;x_{i,} y)$$

$L(w;x_{i,} y) = \frac{1}{2}(w^T x - y)^2$ and $R(w)$ is the regularizer factor.

The minimum can be here identified by using the stochastic gradient descend or with other more advanced methodologies which are outside the scope of this introductory book.

The code below is an example of Spark for Linear Regression. This image represents an example of linear regression and related regression line.

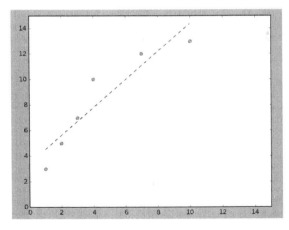

Code

```
from pyspark.mllib.regression import LabeledPoint, LinearRegressionWithSGD
from numpy import array
```

```
# parse the point into a LabeledPoint
#  made up of (label, set of features)
def parsePoint(line):
    values = [float(x) for x in line.replace(',', ' ').split(' ')]
    return LabeledPoint(values[0], values[1:])

# load the data into a resilient distributed data (RDD)
data = sc.textFile("data/mllib/ridge-data/lpsa.data")

#trasform the RDD into an RDD of LabeledPoint
parsedData = data.map(parsePoint)

# Build the model by training a linear regression on the parsedData
model = LinearRegressionWithSGD.train(parsedData)

# Evaluate the model on training data
# We are creating an RDD of pairs (label, prediction) via a lambda call
valuesAndPreds = parsedData.map(lambda p: (p.label, model.predict(p.features)))

# compute the MSE by mapping the label and prediction into the squared diff
# then reduce the distributed differences by summing them
# spark collects all the intermediate results via reduction
# this value is then divided by the total number of (label, prediction) tuples
MSE = valuesAndPreds.map(lambda (v, p): (v - p)**2).reduce(lambda x, y: x +
y) / valuesAndPreds.count()
print("Mean Squared Error = " + str(MSE))
```

41. What are Lasso, Ridge, and ElasticNet regularizations?

Solution

Linear least squares method uses no regularization. Ridge regression uses L2 regularizations and Lasso uses L1 regularization. Both Lasso and Ridge produce coefficients for the learned model that are smaller than the version of regression with no regularization. However, Lasso tends to produce more zero coefficients, thus increasing the model sparsity and its compactness. Sometimes Ridge and Lasso are used together and those are the so-called ElasticNet models.

42.What is a Logistic Regression?

Solution

A "Logistic Regression" is the problem of finding $\min_{w \in R^k} f(w)$, where the objective function is a loss function

$$L(w;x_i, y) = log(1 + e^{-yw^T x})$$

Each prediction is made by using a logistic function $f(h) = \dfrac{1}{1 + e^{-h}}$, where $h = w^T x$ for each new unseen observation x. Logistic regressions are widely used to predict binary responses. If $(w^T x) > 0.5$, then the outcome is positive, otherwise the outcome is negative. In other words, by thresholding the result is possible to use Logistic Regression for binary classification. For instance, this technique is frequently used for predicting the click on web links or ads also because it is very fast to be computed once the model is built.

A variant of logistic regression is the multinomial one which can predict K different outcomes, where one class is used as pivot and all the other ones are chosen in turn against the pivot. In other words, $K - 1$ models are run and the one with higher probability is picked as prediction.

Stochastic or mini-batch Gradient descents can be used for solving logistic regression problems.

The following spark code is very similar to the one presented for linear regression and indeed the only difference here is the class used to learn models.

Code

```python
from pyspark.mllib.regression import LabeledPoint,
LogisticRegressionWithLBFGS
from numpy import array

# parse the point into a LabeledPoint
# made up of (label, set of features)
def parsePoint(line):
    values = [float(x) for x in line.replace('.', ' ').split(' ')]
    return LabeledPoint(values[0], values[1:])
```

```
# load the data into a resilient distributed data (RDD)
data = sc.textFile("data/mllib/ridge-data/lpsa.data")

#trasform the RDD into an RDD of LabeledPoint
parsedData = data.map(parsePoint)

# Build the model by training a linear regression on the parsedData
model = LogisticRegressionWithLBFGS.train(parsedData)

# Evaluate the model on training data
# We are creating an RDD of pairs (label, prediction) via a lambda call
valuesAndPreds = parsedData.map(lambda p: (p.label, model.predict(p.features)))

# compute the MSE by reducing the squared difference between label and
prediction
# then we reduce the distributed differences by summing them
# spark collects all the intermediate results via reduction
# this value is then divided by the total number of (label, prediction) tuples
MSE = valuesAndPreds.map(lambda (v, p): (v - p)**2).reduce(lambda x, y: x +
y) / valuesAndPreds.count()
print("Mean Squared Error = " + str(MSE))
```

43.What is a stepwise regression?

Solution

In a stepwise selection the choice of predictive variables is automatically carried out by exploring the space of features. Stepwise regression can reduce the risk of overfitting and can help to find a simple model with good performances but it can be very expensive. This is particularly true if the feature space is explored brute-force with no additional hints on how to pick the right set of features. There are three variants of stepwise regression:

- **Forward selection**, which starts with no features in the model, tests the addition of each feature using some error estimation and adds the variable only if it improves the model. The selection is repeated until no feature improves the model
- **Backward elimination**, which starts with all candidate features, tests the deletion of each feature using some error estimation and then deletes the variable that improves the model the most after being

deleted. This elimination is repeated until no feature deletion improves the model

- **Bidirectional elimination**, which combines the previous two steps together.

44.How to include nonlinear information into linear models

Solution

Linear methods are created to make forecasts as a linear combination of features. However, if the data is inherently not linearly separable, then it is still possible to use linear models in a few situations. The key idea is to approximate nonlinearities in the problem as features polynomials. This is the so called basis expansion. As an example, if you believe that one feature can have quadratic impact on the forecast, then you can add the square of the feature to the feature space. Picking the right basis expansion for the right set of features is an art which requires a lot of fine-tuning and experience. We will see another example of this technique when we will discuss about the SVM trick.

Linear and non linear separable data

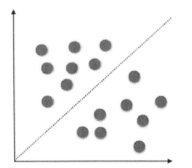 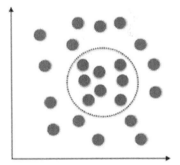

45.What is a Naïve Bayes classifier?

Solution

A naïve Bayes classifier is a machine learning methodology which assigns class labels to each instance of real application data. The naïve attribute is related to the assumption that each feature provides a probabilistic contribution to the learned model, which is independent from the other features.

For instance a text article can be assigned to the category "sports" because it contains the word °*first*°, independently from the fact that it also contains the word °*base*°. These two words are considered separately but not in correlation. Despite their naive scheme and apparently simplified assumptions, naïve Bayes classifiers have worked quite well in many difficult and practical situations.

Mathematically the problem can be formulated by considering an instance observation characterized by means of a suitable vector of n features $X = (x_1,..., x_n)$ where the goal is to assign the best class probability $C_k \in (C_1...,$ $C_j)$ conditioned to the observation of X. This is statistically described as $PR(C_k \mid X)$ and the Bayes theorem[20] allows to estimate this probability as follows:

$$PR(C_k \mid X) = \frac{PR(C_k)\,PR(X \mid C_k)}{PR(X)}$$

According to this theorem the *posterior* probability of assigning class C_k given the observation of X is equal to the *prior* probability of observing class C_k in the training set, multiplied by the *likelihood* of observing X conditioned to the observation of class C_k in the training set, divided by the probability of observing X in it. In other words this posterior prediction can be formulated in terms of observations in the training set.

In plain English:

$$Posterior = \frac{prior * likelihood}{evidence}$$

Now let's focus on each single equation component: $PR(X)$ is a constant scaling factor which will not influence the respective rank of each predicted category, so it can be safely ignored. $PR(C_k)$ can be estimated for instance by considering the frequency of each category in the training set.

---

[20] https://en.wikipedia.org/wiki/Bayes%27_theorem

$$PR(C_k) = \frac{number\ of\ samples\ in\ the\ class}{total\ number\ of\ samples}$$

The estimation of $PR(X|C_k)$ can be done by using the chaining rule[21] which permits the calculation of any member of the joint distribution of a set of random variables using only conditional probabilities.

$$PR(X|C_k) = PR(x_1, ..., x_n|C_k) =$$

$$PR(x_1|C_k)PR(x_2, ..., x_n|C_k, x_1) =$$

$$PR(x_1|C_k)PR(x_2|C_k, x_1)PR(x_3, ..., x_n|C_k, x_1, x_2) =$$

$$PR(x_1|C_k)\ PR(x_2|C_k, x_1)...\ PR(x_n|C_k, x_1, x_2, ..., x_{n-1})$$

The naïve assumption is that each feature is independent from all the remaining ones. So under this assumption:

$$PR(x_1|C_k)\ PR(x_2|C_k, x_1)...\ PR(x_n|C_k, x_1, x_2, ..., x_{n-1})$$

$$= PR(x_1|C_k)PR(x_2|C_k)...PR(x_n|C_k)$$

And the Naive Bayes Classifier becomes very simple

$$PR(C_k|X) \propto PR(C_k) \prod_{i=1}^{n} PR(x_i|C_k)$$

Where the symbol $\propto$ denotes proportionality.

In short all categories are evaluated against the above formula and we pick just the one maximizing it:

$$\hat{c} = \underset{k}{\operatorname{argmax}}\ PR(C_k) \prod_{i=1}^{n} PR(x_i|C_k)$$

Note that multiplying small probabilities in $[0,1]$ can be problematic, so usually it is more convenient to operate in a log-space by using a well-known algebraic property of logarithms $a * b = e^{\ln(a*b)} = e^{\ln(a)+\ln(b)}$.

In order to estimate $PR(x_i|C_k)$, we should distinguish between discrete training data (for instance the features used for textual classification) and continuous training data (for instance: the features used for image

---

[21] https://en.wikipedia.org/wiki/Chain_rule_(probability)

classification that might be continuous). The former one can be modelled using Bernoulli or Multinomial distributions, while the latter one is typically modelled using Gaussians.

46. What is a Bernoulli and a Multivariate Naïve Bayes?

Solution

In Bernoulli all features are simple binary variables describing the presence or absence of one particular attribute in the observed training set. Therefore, Bernoulli can be modelled as

$$PR(x_i|\ C_k) = \prod_{i=1}^{n} p_{ki}^{x_i}(1 - p_{ki}^{x_i})^{(1 - x_i)}$$

where $p_{ki}^{x_i}$ is the probability of observing feature x_i in class C_k. Bernoulli is frequently used for text classification by explicitly modelling the presence or the absence of a word term w_i in the text.

A multivariate is a variant of Bernoulli, where x_i counts the number of times an event was observed in a particular instance. Multivariates are very popular for text classifications where the text is represented by an independent collection of words: the so called bag of words. The likelihood of observing a word is mathematically expressed by

$$PR(x_i|\ C_k) = \frac{\left(\sum_{i=1}^{n} x_i \right)!}{\prod_{l=1}^{n} x_i!} \prod_{i=1}^{n} p_{ki}^{x_i}$$

Again, when computing small probabilities in $[0,1]$, it is better to move into the log-space, so that ignoring the constant scaling factors we have

$$log(PR(\ C_k\ |\ X)) \propto log(PR(\ C_k) \prod_{i=1}^{n} PR(x_i|\ C_k)) = log(PR(\ C_k)) + \sum_{i=1}^{n} x_i log p_{ki}^{x_i}$$

Note that the latter one is a simple linear form of $b + w_k^T x$ with $b = log(PR(C_k))$ and $w_{ki} = x_i log p_{ki}$. Also note that with this formulation if a probability is zero, this will wipe all other contributions. This problem is solved with the so called smoothing strategy, where some small constant factors are used to replace zero.

The code here below uses Spark to train a multinomial Bayes classifier on text data. The metric adopted for evaluating quality is accuracy, which is the number of correct predictions made, divided by the total number of predictions made and multiplied by 100 to turn it into a percentage. Accuracy is calculated by using a map-reduce computation on Spark. Note that the dataset has been split in training (70% of the data) and test (30% of the data). The smoothing factor is set to 1.0.

Code

```
from pyspark.mllib.classification import NaiveBayes
from pyspark.mllib.linalg import Vectors
from pyspark.mllib.regression import LabeledPoint

# create an appopriate LabeledPoint of tuples (label, features)
def parseLine(line):
    parts = line.split('.')
    label = float(parts[0])
    features = Vectors.dense([float(x) for x in parts[1].split(' ')])
    return LabeledPoint(label, features)

#create an RDD from the text file made up of LabeledPoint
data = sc.textFile('data/mllib/sample_naive_bayes_data.txt').map(parseLine)

# Split data into training (70%) and test (30%)
# Fix the seed for reproducipility of the experiment
training, test = data.randomSplit([0.7, 0.3], seed = 0)

# Train a multinomial naive Bayes with smoothing factor 1.0
model = NaiveBayes.train(training, 1.0)

# Make prediction and test accuracy
predictionAndLabel = test.map(lambda p : (model.predict(p.features), p.label))
accuracy = 1.0 * predictionAndLabel.filter(lambda (x, v): x == v).count() / test.count()
```

47.What is a Gaussian?

Solution

A Gaussian is a family of mathematical functions which shows a characteristic symmetric "bell curve" shape. Mathematically: given the mean μ and the variance σ, a Gaussian is defined as

$$N(\mu, \sigma^2, x) = \frac{1}{\sqrt{2\pi\sigma^2}} e^{-\frac{(x-\mu)^2}{2\sigma^2}}$$

The Gaussian distribution is a very common continuous probability distribution frequently used in statistics because of the **Central Limit Theorem**. This theorem states that average random variables independently drawn from independent distributions (also known as i.i.d.) are normally distributed.

The simplest case of normal distribution is $N(1, 0)$. In the following examples 500 random numbers are sampled with $N(0, 1)$ and associated to buckets. The drawn values have the classical bell shape. The function has its peak at the mean and the "spread" increases by increasing the standard deviation σ.

Code

```
import matplotlib.pyplot as plt
import numpy as np
mu, sigma = 0, 1 # mean and standard deviation
s = np.random.normal(mu, sigma, 500)
count, bins, ignored = plt.hist(s, 50, normed=True)
plt.plot(bins, 1/(sigma * np.sqrt(2 * np.pi)) *
         np.exp( - (bins - mu)**2 / (2 * sigma**2) ),
         linewidth=2, color='r')
plt.show()
```

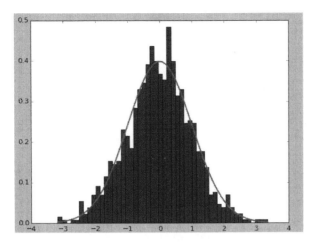

As an exercise try to plot the image for different values of σ and remark the differences.

48. What is a Standard Scaling?

Solution

If a data is described by a Gaussian then it might be convenient to transform it by scaling its features to unit variance and/or removing the mean using column summary statistics on the samples in the training set. The code here below implements the scaling to unit variance and the removing of the mean in Spark.

Code

```
from pyspark.mllib.util import MLUtils
from pyspark.mllib.linalg import Vectors
from pyspark.mllib.feature import StandardScaler

data = MLUtils.loadLibSVMFile(sc, "data/mllib/sample libsvm data.txt")
label = data.map(lambda x: x.label)
features = data.map(lambda x: x.features)

scaler1 = StandardScaler().fit(features)
scaler2 = StandardScaler(withMean=True, withStd=True).fit(features)
scaler3 = StandardScalerModel(scaler2.std, scaler2.mean)

# data1 is scaled to the unit variance
data1 = label.zip(scaler1.transform(features))
```

```
# data2 is scaled to the unit variance and has zero mean.
data2 = label.zip(scaler1.transform(features.map(lambda x:
Vectors.dense(x.toArray()))))
# features are mapped into dense vectors, for avoiding exceptions
# for transformation with zero mean on sparse vector.
```

49. Why are statistical distributions important?

Solution

Statistical distributions are important for modelling events and data. Distributions are characterized by functions such as the *probability mass function (pmf)*, which provides the probability that a discrete random variable is exactly equal to some value, and the *cumulative distribution function (CDF)*, which describes the probability of a real-valued random variable X to have a value less than or equal to x. In addition to the Normal ones the following distributions are frequently used in Data Science:

	What	**PMF**	**CMF**	**E(X)**	**VAR(X)**
Bernoulli	A discrete distribution. It takes value 1 with p probability and value 0 with probability $q = 1 - p$. A classic example is a single toss of a coin.	$f(k,p) = \begin{cases} p, & k = 1 \\ q = 1 - p, & k = 0 \end{cases}$ $f(k,p) = p^k (1-p)^{(1-k)}$	$\begin{cases} 0 & k < 0 \\ q & 0 \le k \le 1 \\ 1 & k \ge 1 \end{cases}$	p	pq

Binomial	A discrete distribution. It describes the number of successes in a series of independent yes/no experiments all with the same probability of success.	$f(n,k,p) = \binom{n}{k} p^k (1-p)^{(1}$ n, number of trials k, number of successes p, probability of success in each trial where $\binom{n}{k} = \dfrac{n!}{k!(n-k)!}$	$F(n,k,p) =$ $Pr(X \leq k) =$ $\displaystyle\sum_{i=0}^{\lfloor k \rfloor} \binom{n}{i} p^i (1-p)^{(n-i)}$	np	$np(1-p)$
Poisson binomial	It describes the number of successes in a series of independent Yes/No experiments with different probabilities of success	$\displaystyle\sum_{A \in F^K} \prod_{i \in A} p_i \prod_{i \in A^C}(1-p_j)$ where F^K is the set of all subsets of k integers that can be selected from {1,2,3,...,n}. A^C is the complement of set A.	$\displaystyle\sum_{l=0}^{k} \sum_{A \in F^K} \prod_{i \in A} p_i \prod_{j \in A^C} q_j$ where $q_j = (1-p_j)$	$\displaystyle\sum_{i=1}^{n} p_i$	$\sigma^2 =$ $\displaystyle\sum_{i=1}^{n} q_i p_i$
Poisson	A discrete distribution. It describes the probability of events in a fixed interval of time / space with a known average rate arriving independently from time since the last event.	$f(k,\lambda) =$ $Pr\,(X = k) =$ $\dfrac{\lambda^k}{k!} e^{-\lambda}$ The positive real number λ is the expected value of the random variable X and also of its variance. K is an integer	$e^{-\lambda} \displaystyle\sum_{i=0}^{\lfloor k \rfloor} \dfrac{\lambda^i}{i!}$	λ	λ

| Gaussian | A distribution on real. The central limit theorem: every variable modelled as a sum of many i.i.d, variables with finite mean, variance is normal. | $N(\mu, \sigma^2, x) = \dfrac{1}{\sqrt{2\pi\sigma^2}} e^{-\frac{(x-\mu)^2}{2\sigma^2}}$ | $\dfrac{1}{2}\left[1 + erf(\dfrac{x-\mu}{\sigma\sqrt{2}})\right]$ | μ | σ^2 |

Code

Numpy provides full support for all the distributions described above and many others more. The interested reader is encouraged to check them on Wikipedia.[22]

```
import numpy as np
n, p = 10, .5 # number of trials, probability of each trial
s = np.random.binomial(n, p, 100)
print s
```

50.Can you compare your data with some distribution? What is a qq-plot?

Solution

If you want to investigate whether your data follow some distribution (normal, uniform), one useful way is to use a qq-plot, which can compare two probability distributions by plotting their quantiles against each other. If the distributions are similar, then the graph will show a straight line.

Code

```
import numpy as np
import pylab
import scipy.stats as stats
```

---

[22] https://en.wikipedia.org/wiki/List_of_probability_distributions

```
measurements = np.random.normal(loc = 40, scale = 10, size=80)
stats.probplot(measurements, dist="norm", plot=pylab)
pylab.show()
```

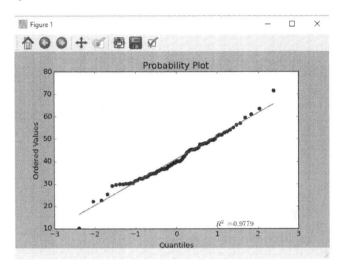

51.What is a Gaussian Naïve Bayes?

Solution

If the data is continuous, it might be convenient to estimate the probability by using a Gaussian distribution. So if feature x_i is continuous, we compute the mean $\mu_{C_K}^{x_i}$ and the variance $\sigma_{C_K}^{x_i}$ of x_i in C_K, then we model the probabilities as Gaussians in this way:

$$PR(X = x \mid C) = \frac{1}{\sqrt{2\pi\sigma^2}} e^{-\frac{(x-\mu)^2}{2\sigma^2}}$$

As discussed, it could be useful to check whether our data is indeed showing a Gaussian distribution by using tools such as qq-plot.

52.What is another way to use Naïve Bayes with continuous data?

Another approach for dealing with continuous features is to discretize them in buckets and use Multinomial Naïve Bayes for the discrete model. However some attention should be put in place for determining the right number of buckets.

53.What is the Nearest Neighbor classification?

Solution

A "nearest neighbor" is a very simple form of classification where each instance is assigned to the objects which are closer to the instance. During the training phase the space of features is partitioned in regions according to the position of the training instances. Then during the application phase the distance with respect to the training instances is used to classify real data.

There are many choices that can be made. For instance we can consider the closest object or we consider up to k objects and let them vote to pick the winning class. This is the so called k-NN classifier. Also we might define different types of vectorial distances. Given two vectors $P = (p_1, ...,p_n)$ and $Q = (q_1, ..., q_n)$

	Formula	Description	Visually
Euclidean	$\sqrt{\sum_{i=1}^{n}(q_i - p_i)^2} =$	The Euclidean formula represents the intuitive notion of distance of two points in space.	

Manhattan	$$\sum_{i=1}^{n} |q_i - p_i| = ||P$$	"Manhattan" intuitively maps all the points into a squared grid (similar to the Manhattan map) and the connections can only happen either vertically or horizontally	
Hamming	$\#(q_i \neq p_i)$	Number of positions where the single vector components are different.	2473996 2233796 Have distance 3
Jaccard	$$d(A, B) = \frac{|A \cap B|}{|A \cup B|}$$	Jaccard distance represents the similarity between two sets	$A = \{1,2,3,5\}$ $B = \{1,2,3,6\}$ $d(A,B) = \frac{3}{5}$

Implementing the exact nearest neighbor can be very expensive. Therefore many approximate variants have been proposed, which are generally based on the idea of sampling the feature of space. The interested reader can find here an experimental alpha implementation for Spark.[23]

The code snippet implements here a simple version of Knn where K=1. More sophisticate implementations are based on advanced data structures such as KD-Trees.[24]

Code

```python
import numpy as np

def dist(p0, p1):
    return np.sum((p0-p1)**2)

def knn(training, trainingLabels, newPoint):
    dists = np.array([distance(t, newPoint)] for t in training)
    nearest = dists.argmin()
    return trainingLabels[nearest]
```

[23] https://issues.apache.org/jira/browse/SPARK-2336

[24] https://en.wikipedia.org/wiki/K-d_tree

54.What are Support Vector Machines (SVM)?

Solution

Support vector machines aim to identify a hyperplane in a high dimensional space of features. Intuitively the best hyperplane is the one having the largest distance to the nearest data point observed in any training data. In fact this hyperplane provides the best separation among the training data. The image below provides a toy example where in R^2 line H_1 does not provide any separation between the training data, while e line H_2 provides a non optimal separation. Instead H_3 provides the maximum separation margin.

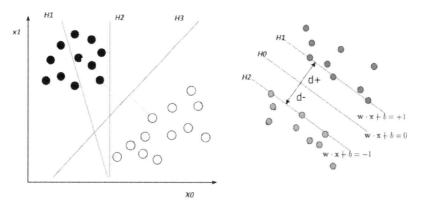

Mathematically let us assume to have a training set made of pairs of features and true binary labels: $\{(X_i, y_i)|X \in R^k,\ y_i \in \{-1, +1\}\}$ and let us assume that the data here can be linearly separated by a hyperplane, which is described by the linear relation $w^T x - b = 0$ for a suitable weight vector w. Let us consider two additional hyperplanes: one for the positive examples $w^T x - b = 1$ and one for the negative examples $w^T x - b = -1$.

Recalling the distance from a point (x_0, y_0) to a line: $Ax + By + c = 0$ is $\dfrac{|Ax_0 + By_0 + c|}{\sqrt{A^2 + B^2}}$ and as consequence the distance between H_0 and H_1 is then $\dfrac{|w^T x - b|}{||w||} = \dfrac{1}{||w||}$.

Therefore the total distance between H_1 and H_2 is $\dfrac{2}{||w||}$ and for minimizing the distance we need to maximize the $||w||$. However we also want that no data point touches the margins which can be expressed as

$$\begin{cases} w^T x - b \geq 1 & y = 1 \\ w^T x - b \leq -1 & y = -1 \end{cases} \rightarrow y(w^T x - b \geq 1).$$

More synthetically we want to solve the optimization problem

$$\min_{(w,b)} ||w|| \text{ under the constrains } y_i(w^T x_i - b \geq 1)$$

Since the square root is a monotonic function, we can more conveniently solve the problem in this way:

$$\min_{(w,b)} \frac{1}{2}||w||^2 \text{ under the constrains } y_i(w^T x_i - b \geq 1)$$

Fortunately there are packages which can solve this optimization problem with advanced mathematical tools. For instance: Spark implements SVM with hinge loss function $L(w; x_i, y) = max\{0, 1 - y w^T x\}$, regularization of type L1 or L2. The optimization problem is solved by using the Stochastic Gradient Descent.

Once the model is learned, the prediction is simply a vector multiplication. For each application instance x_a if $w^T x_a \geq 0$ the outcome is positive, otherwise it is negative.

Note that the data points in each class lying closest to the classification line are called "support vectors" and they are the reason for the name of this methodology.

Code

```
from pyspark.mllib.classification import SVMWithSGD, SVMModel
from pyspark.mllib.regression import LabeledPoint

# Load and parse the data into LabeledPoint
def parsePoint(line):
    values = [float(x) for x in line.split(' ')]
    return LabeledPoint(values[0], values[1:])

data = sc.textFile("data/mllib/sample_svm_data.txt")
parsedData = data.map(parsePoint)
```

```
# Build the model for SVM with Stocastic Gradient Descent
model = SVMWithSGD.train(parsedData, iterations=100)

# Evaluating the model on training data
labelsAndPreds = parsedData.map(lambda p: (p.label, model.predict(p.features)))
# Compute the accuracy
trainErr = labelsAndPreds.filter(lambda (v, p): v != p).count() /
float(parsedData.count())
print("Training Error = " + str(trainErr))
```

55.What are SVM Kernel tricks?

Solution

If a linear separation is not enough, then it is still possible to use SVM with simple tricks. For example, if the original data consists of 3-dimensional vectors [x, y, z] , then we could compute a new 9-dimensional feature vector $[x, y, z, x^2, y^2, z^2, xy, xz, yz]$. This basic idea can be extended as explained in "*Random Features for Large-Scale Kernel Machines*"[25]. The intuition here is that Kernel methods *remember* the i-th training example (x_i, y) and combine it with a another training example.

In certain situations an additional structure is added and the kernel is a special function which maps the input space Ψ into another space Ω so that $\varphi: \Psi \rightarrow \Omega$ and the Kernel is an inner product between $\varphi(x)$ and (y) , where two features x, y are provided from the original input space. In other words a kernel function maps a non-linear boundary in the problem space to a linear boundary in a higher dimensional space.

---

[25]http://www.eecs.berkeley.edu/~brecht/papers/07.rah.rec.nips.pdf

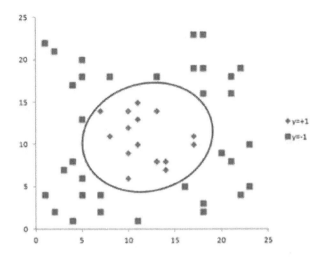

These are examples of kernels frequently used in machine learning

Examples of kernels	Meaning
$K(x, y) = (1 + xy)^s$	Polynomial for some degrees s
$K(x, y) = tanh(kxy - h)$	Sigmoid for some parameters k, h
$K(x, y) = e^{\frac{-(x-y)^2}{2\sigma^2}}$	Radial basis for some parameters σ

56. What is K-Means Clustering?

Solution

K-means is a form of flat clustering where the goal is to partition space into a set of groups without creating relations among them. In the next volume we will present a form of hierarchical clustering where the groups are organized in a hierarchical tree.

K-Means is a form of unsupervised learning, where the actual data is grouped in K different clusters. Mathematically: given N observations $(X_1, .., X_n)$, where each observation is a vector of d features $X_i \epsilon R^d$, K-means method partitions the N observations in $K \leq N$ sets $S = (S_1,...,S_K)$ in such a way that the within-cluster error expressed as sum of squares is minimized

$$\underset{S}{\operatorname{argmin}} \sum_{i=1}^{n} \sum_{x \epsilon S_i} ||x - \mu_i||^2$$

An approximate solution to the problem is computed iteratively. The algorithm starts by randomly picking K points in $X_i \epsilon R^d$, the so-called centroids. Then alternatively two steps are repeated until either a convergence or a stopping criteria is met. First, each observation is assigned to the group, the centroid of which has the least within-cluster sum of squares from the observation. Then the mean for each group is updated by considering the observations laying within the group. The algorithm has converged when the assignments no longer change. Since both steps optimize the infra-cluster distance and only a finite number of such partitions exists, the algorithm must converge to a (local) optimum.

K-Means++ is a variant of K-Means where the initial K clusters are spread out: the first cluster center is chosen uniformly at random from the application data points, after which each successive cluster center is chosen from the remaining data points with a probability that is proportional to its squared distance from the closest existing cluster center point. Spark implements a variant of K-Means++ called K-Means||[26] , suitable for parallel computation.

Code

```
from pyspark.mllib.clustering import KMeans, KMeansModel
from numpy import array
from math import sqrt


# Load and parse the data into an appropriate RDD
data = sc.textFile("data/mllib/kmeans_data.txt")
parsedData = data.map(lambda line: array([float(x) for x in line.split(' ')]))

# Build the model for a maxIterations=10
# and with 10 runs, with random centroid
```

---

[26] http://spark.apache.org/docs/latest/mllib-clustering.html#k-means

```
clusters = KMeans.train(parsedData, 2, maxIterations=10,
    runs=10, initializationMode="random")

# Evaluate clustering by computing Within Set Sum of Squared Errors
def error(point):
    center = clusters.centers[clusters.predict(point)]
    return sqrt(sum([x**2 for x in (point - center)]))

# each point is mapped into the error and all the errors are summed
WSSSE = parsedData.map(lambda point: error(point)).reduce(lambda x, y: x +
y)
print("Within Set Sum of Squared Error = " + str(WSSSE))
```

57. Can you provide an example for Text Classification with Spark?

Solution

Let's discuss about Text Classification in Spark and leverage multiple techniques introduced in previous questions. In this example textual words are loaded and transformed into a vector space. Then the examples are split (70%, 30%) into training and test datasets where a Naïve Bayes model is learned. The error metric adopted is accuracy.

Code

```
from pyspark import SparkContext, SparkConf
from pyspark.mllib.feature import HashingTF
from pyspark.mllib.regression import LabeledPoint
from pyspark.mllib.classification import NaiveBayes
conf = SparkConf().setMaster("local[*]").setAppName("Naive_Bayes")
sc = SparkContext(conf=conf)

# Hash words a discrete vector space
# with the limit of 10000 words
htf = HashingTF(10000)

#tokenize sentences and transform them into vector space model

# examples
dataRDD = sc.textFile("./positiveData.txt")
data = dataRDD.map(lambda text : LabeledPoint(1, htf.transform(text.split(" "))))
data.persist()

# Build training and test data sets for examples
```

```
# Training set is 70% of data, while test set is 30% of data
trainData, testData = data.randomSplit([0.7, 0.3])

# Train a Naive Bayes model on the training data
model = NaiveBayes.train(trainData)

# Compare predicted labels to actual labels
prediction_and_labels = testData.map(lambda point:
(model.predict(point.features), point.label))

# Filter to only correct predictions
correct = prediction_and_labels.filter(lambda (predicted, actual): predicted ==
actual)

# Calculate and print accuracy rate
accuracy = correct.count() / float(testh.count())

print "Classifier correctly predicted category " + str(accuracy * 100) + " percent
of the time"
```

58. Where to go from here

The best next step is to start playing with real data and applying the algorithms presented in this volume. Kaggle[27] is a platform for data prediction in competitions. Companies, organizations and researchers post their data and have it scrutinized by the best experts worldwide. So you can go there and run few competitions for showcasing your value!

Remember: great machine learning results can be achieved by finding the right mix among the steps described in the below image.

Every problem is represented by means of observed data. Data is noisy. So you need to select the right summaries via feature engineering along with the appropriate algorithm for learning. At the same time it is certainly useful to provide a good mathematical formulation to the machine learning problem. Then it is a matter of training (for supervised learning) and evaluation. For supervised learning a good gold set can help. The process is iterative: when you reach satisfying results or when you are stuck and don't make any progress, that is exactly the right moment for iterating and improving, trying to refine and frequently re-assess all the choices made so far. After a few

[27] https://www.kaggle.com/

iterations you might be satisfied of your results and deploy the model online for making forecasts on real unseen data. Users will provide you with feedback (either explicit or implicit) and those are new signals that you might want to collect for further refining your models.

A great Data scientist always works in incremental and lean way!!!

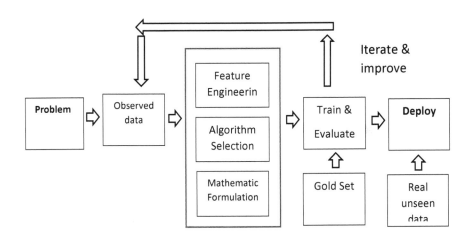

I hope that this first volume provided you with some basic tools for machine learning and also reduced the halo of mystery surrounding the role of Data science (after all it is all about data, math, coding and lots of creativity!). The second volume will discuss in more details more advanced topics such as decision trees, random forests, mars, gradient boosted trees, ensembles, hyper-parameters search, density estimation, expectation-maximization, dimensional reduction, bagging, recommendations, neural networks, deep learning and associative rules.

Appendix A

59. Ultra-Quick introduction to Python

I assume that you are already familiar with programming languages and hopefully you already have some experience with Python. However it is useful to recall some peculiarities of the languages which are used in this book.

Python does not use { } for delimiting code blocks but instead it uses indentation, which can be confusing at the beginning if you are used to C/C++ programming. Importing a module and defining a function have a simple syntax

```
import numpy as np

def dist(p0, p1):
    return np.sum((p0-p1)**2)
```

Lists are defined with square brackets and slicing operations are easily supported.

```
l=[1,2,3,4,5]

x[:3] #first three
x[3:] #three to end
x[2:4] #2nd, 3rd, 4th
y = x[:] #copy
```

List comprehension is useful for transforming a list into another list by selecting some elements or by transforming other elements with a suitable function. This example creates a list of 100 tuples $[(0, 0), (0,1), ... (100, 100)]$

```
pairs = [(x, y) for x in range(10) for y in range(10)]
```

Python supports anonymous functions also known as lambda computation. This is frequently used in Spark as reported in this example:

```
# map reduce
textFile.map(lambda line: len(line.split())).reduce(lambda a, b: a if (a > b) else b)
```

Numpy is a library for efficient linear algebra and numerical computation. In this book we used numpy vectors intensively.

```
import numpy as np

def dist(p0, p1):
    return np.sum((p0-p1)**2)

def knn(training, trainingLabels, newPoint):
    dists = np.array([distance(t, newPoint)] for t in training)
    nearest = dists.argmin()
    return trainingLabels[nearest]
```

Anaconda is a very convenient Python distribution for Data Science.[28]

60.Ultra-Quick introduction to Probabilities

Probabilities can be seen as a way to quantify the uncertainty for an event E from a universe of events. Mathematically this is denoted with $P(E)$. Two events E, F are independent if the probability of having both of them happening is $P(E, F) = P(E)P(F)$. If the events are not independent, then $(E, F) = P(E \mid F)P(F)$, which means that the joint probability is equal to the conditional probability of seeing E given the F, times the probability of F.

The Bayes theorem is a powerful tool for learning because it allows to *reverse* conditional probabilities. Mathematically the theorem states that:

$$P(E \mid F) = \frac{P(E, F)}{P(F)} \underset{Bayes}{=} \frac{P(F \mid E)P(E)}{P(F)}$$

61.Ultra-Quick introduction to Matrices and Vectors

Vectors of length n represent points in an n-dimensional space. Vectors are typically represented with the notation x_i with $i = 1,...,n$ and sometimes with bold letters x when there is no ambiguity. Matrices are tables with rows and columns. They are typically represented as $A_{i,j}$ and when there is no ambiguity as **A**. The transpose of a matrix $A_{i,j}$ is $A_{j,i}$ and it is denoted as A^T. The transpose of a vector x of dimension n × 1 is the same vector 1 × n.

---

[28] https://store.continuum.io/cshop/anaconda/

Given a vector **x,** we define the norm $$||x||_p = (\sum_{i=1}^{n} |x_i|^p)^{\frac{1}{p}}$$ and $||x||_\infty = max(|x_1|, \dots, |x_n|)$

Given two vectors x, **y**, the inner product $$x\,y = \sum_{i=1}^{n} x_i y_i$$. Given the inner product, we define the cosine similarity as $$\cos(\theta) = \frac{xy}{(xx)(yy)} = \frac{xy}{||x||||y||},$$ where θ is the angle between the vectors represented by x and y.

Given two vectors **x, y,** the outer product $x \otimes y$ is equivalent to a matrix multiplication xy^T, provided that x is represented as a $m \times 1$ column vector and y as an n × 1 column vector.

$$a \otimes b = ab^T = \begin{bmatrix} a_1b_1 & \cdots & a_1b_n \\ \vdots & \ddots & \vdots \\ a_nb_1 & \cdots & a_nb_n \end{bmatrix}$$

ABOUT THE AUTHOR

An experienced data mining engineer, passionate about technology and innovation in consumers' space. Interested in search and machine learning on massive dataset with a particular focus on query analysis, suggestions, entities, personalization, freshness and universal ranking. Antonio Gulli has worked in small startups, medium (Ask.com, Tiscali) and large corporations (Microsoft, RELX). His carrier path is about mixing industry with academic experience.

Antonio holds a Master Degree in Computer Science and a Master Degree in Engineering, and a Ph.D. in Computer Science. He founded two startups, one of them was one of the earliest search engine in Europe back in 1998. He filed more than 20 patents in search, machine learning and distributed system. Antonio wrote several books on algorithms and currently he serves as (Senior) Program Committee member in many international conferences. Antonio teaches also computer science and video game programming to hundreds of youngsters on a voluntary basis.

"Nowadays, you must have a great combination of research skills and a just-get-it-done attitude."

Made in the USA
San Bernardino, CA
15 September 2016